A Year on the Farm

By Sue Unstead

Series Editor Deborah Lock
US Senior Editor Shannon Beatty
Art Editor Yamini Panwar
Pre-production Editor Francesca Wardell
DTP Designer Anita Yadav, Syed Md Farhan
Picture Researcher Sumedha Chopra
Managing Editor Soma B. Chowdhury
Managing Art Editor Ahlawat Gunjan
Art Director Martin Wilson

Reading Consultant Linda Gambrell

First American Edition, 2015
Published in the United States by DK Publishing
345 Hudson Street, New York, New York 10014

A catalog record for this book is available
from the Library of Congress.
ISBN: 978-1-4654-3577-4 (Paperback)
ISBN: 978-1-4654-3576-7 (Hardcover)

DK books are available at special discounts when purchased in bulk for sales promotions, premiums, fund-raising, or educational use. For details, contact: DK Publishing Special Markets
345 Hudson Street, New York, New York 10014
SpecialSales@dk.com
Printed and bound in China

The publisher would like to thank the following for their kind permission to reproduce their photographs:
(Key: a-above; b-below/bottom; c-center; f-far; l-left; r-right; t-top)
1 Alamy Images: Tatiana Cahill. **7 Getty Images:** Digital Vision. **8 iStockphoto.com:** RMAX (b). **9 Getty Images:** Image Source (r). **10–11 Getty Images:** E+/Jason Titzer (b). **12 Getty Images:** Duncan Davis (br); E+/stocknshares (clb). **13 Getty Images:** Mattias Nilsson (clb); Ronnie Kaufman/Larry Hirshowitz (br). **14 iStockphoto.com:** JacobH (t, b). **15 iStockphoto.com:** JacobH (t, b). **17 Fotolia:** Olena Pantiukh (bc). **19 Corbis:** Cultura/Monty Rakusen (tr). **20 iStockphoto.com:** TheBusman (b). **21 Dreamstime.com:** Orangesquid (cra); Sarah Theophilus (cb); **iStockphoto.com:** martin_33 (crb). **22 Corbis:** Image Source/Sebastian Marmaduke (cla). **24–25 Dorling Kindersley:** The Cotswold Farm Park, Gloucestershire (b). **24 iStockphoto.com:** RMAX. **25 123RF.com:** Francisco De Casa Gonzalez (tr). **26 iStockphoto.com:** ilfede (tl). **26–27 Getty Images:** Vetta/George Clerk (c). **27 Getty Images:** Visuals Unlimited, Inc./Nigel Cattlin (bl). **28–29 Dreamstime.com:** Mike_kiev (b). **29 Corbis:** Cultura / Hybrid Images (r). **30 123RF.com:** martinak (cb/Butter); Sergey Mironov (crb); **Alamy Images:** Valentyn Volkov (cl); **Dreamstime.com:** Robyn Mackenzie (clb); **iStockphoto.com:** vikif (cb/yoghurt). **31 iStockphoto.com:** Lauri Patterson (clb). **32–33 123RF.com:** Jean-Pierre Chretien (b). **33 iStockphoto.com:** tankist276 (c). **34–35 Alamy Images:** Chris Pancewicz. **35 Alamy Images:** imageBROKER/Hartmut Pöstges (br). **36 iStockphoto.com:** jorgeantonio (tl). **36–37 Dreamstime.com:** Marcomayer (b). **38 123RF.com:** jahmaica (cb); **iStockphoto.com:** pkripper503 (cla). **39 123RF.com:** Karol Czinege (tl); Vitaly Suprun (ca); Norman Kin Hang Chan (clb); **Photolibrary:** Digital Vision/Akira Kaede (crb). **42 123RF.com:** Alexey Zarodov (bl); sauletas (crb); **Alamy Images:** Chris Pancewicz (cla).
Jacket images: *Front:* **Dorling Kindersley:** Lister Wilder b. **Fotolia:** Vadim Yerofeyev ca.
Spine: **Corbis:** Peter Mason / cultura.
All other images © Dorling Kindersley
For further information see: www.dkimages.com

A WORLD OF IDEAS:
SEE ALL THERE IS TO KNOW
www.dk.com

Contents

The Farm
Welcome to the farm!

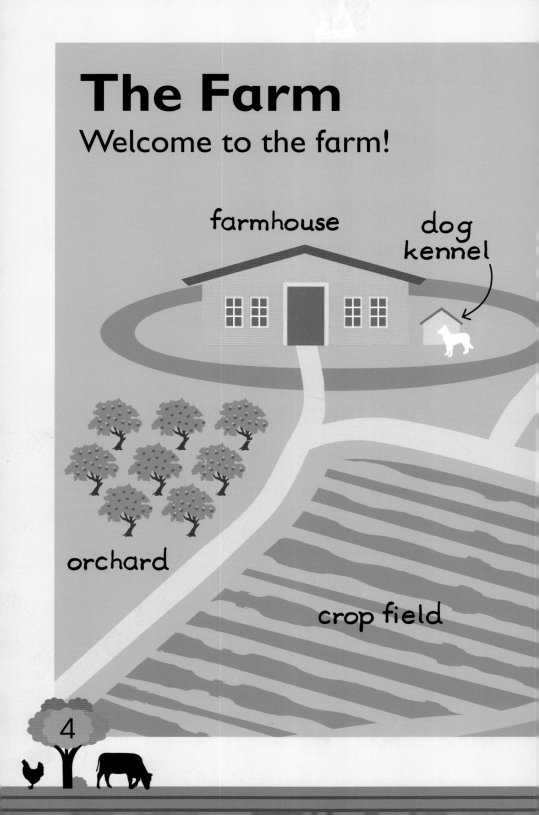

farmhouse

dog kennel

orchard

crop field

field

stable

barn

henhouse

pigsty

crop field

5

Wake Up!

The sun peeks over
the farmyard wall.
**"Cock–a–doodle
doooooo!"**
cries the rooster.
The farmer wakes up.
It's time to get to work.
It's going to be a busy year
on the farm.

Cock-a-doodle dooooo!

Chapter 1
Winter

It is winter.

The farmer's day starts very early in the morning.

It is still dark.

It is time to collect
some eggs.
The farmer and
her dog go out
to see the hens
in the henhouse.
She will take
the eggs to market.

Now the farmer is out
on the farm in the tractor.

Chug, chug, chug...
crunch, splash, splosh.

It is cold and frosty
up on the hill.

Today it is time to get
the fields ready.
Up and down the tractor goes,
churning up the soil.

All day the farmer drives the tractor in the field, turning over the soil.

That was a very long day!
It is time to head home and
put the animals to bed.
The horses are in the stable.
The noisy pigs are in their sty.
The cows are in the barn.
The rooster and the hens are
in the henhouse.

Seasons

These pictures show how a farm changes through the year. What differences do you see?

Winter

Spring

14

Summer

Fall

15

Chapter 2
Spring

It is now spring.
All the animals are very busy
with their babies.

Cheep–cheep!

"Cluck, cluck, cluck," says the hen.
Six fluffy balls of yellow feathers run behind her.
These are her new chicks.
"Cheep—cheep," they cry.

There are four woolly lambs
inside the barn.
"Baa, baa!" they bleat.
One little lamb is lying
in the straw.

Baa, baa!

The farmer picks it up.
She feeds it milk from a bottle.
The milk will help the lamb
grow up to be strong.

The farmer in her tractor
is taking hay to the horses.
A foal is trying out
its wobbly legs.

Now it is time to plant seeds
in the fields:
potatoes in
the little field,
wheat in
the big field,
and peas
by the stream.

Who Am I?

Match the animals to the clues.

1. **Baaa!** My mom is an ewe. My dad is a ram. Who am I?

2. **Oink! Oink!** My mom is a sow. My dad is a boar. Who am I?

3. **Maaaa!** My mom is a nanny. My dad is a billy. Who am I?

4. **Neigh! Neigh!** My mom is a mare. My dad is a stallion. Who am I?

5. **Moo!** My mom is a cow. My dad is a bull. Who am I?

1. Lamb; 2. Piglet; 3. Kid; 4. Foal; 5. Calf.

Chapter 3
Summer

It is summertime.
The farmer takes the tractor
and her dog to the fields.

It is time to round up
the sheep.
The farmer
needs to shear
their woolly coats.
This will keep them cool
in the summer sun.

The farmer has
lots of jobs to do.
First, she goes down
to the stream
to spray the peas.
Spit, sprit, spritzzzz.

Next, she waters the potatoes.
Whoosh, whoosh.

Then she cuts the grass
to make hay.
Chip, chop,
chippety chop.

Now it is time to milk the cow.
"Moo," says the cow,
munching on some
tasty grass.

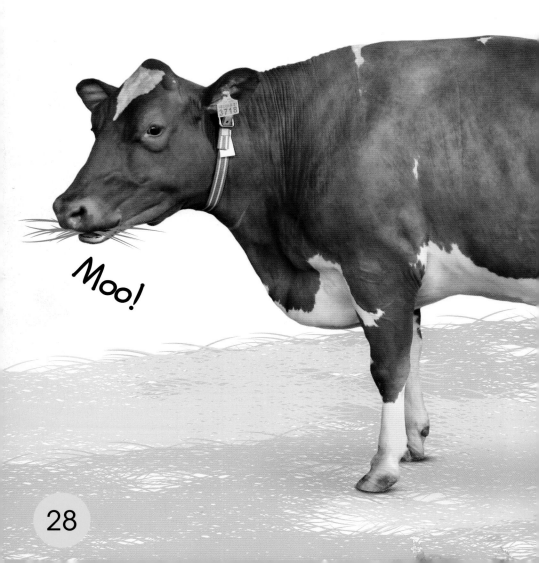

Moo!

The milk is creamy.
It will also be made
into other good things,
like butter and cheese.

Food from the Farm

Farms give us many different foods.

Dairy cows give us milk to drink.
Milk can also be turned into these dairy foods.

cream

butter

Eggs come from hens.

cheese

yogurt

Wheat is made
into flour for bread.

peas

potatoes

apples

31

Chapter 4
Fall

It is now fall.
The farmer drives the tractor
to the big field every day.
She needs to check that
the wheat is ready.

She picks a stalk and
rubs the grain in her fingers.
It is time to cut the wheat.
She goes to get the combine
harvester.

The combine harvester
and the tractor work
in the field all day long.
Swish, swish.

The stalks of wheat are cut as the combine harvester drives through them.

Whoosh, whoosh.
The seeds of grain fall into the hopper.

Roly-poly.
The stalks are rolled into bales of straw.

The farmer picks the apples
in the orchard.
The apples can be used
to make yummy things,
like apple pie and apple cider.

The farmer brings in a box
of potatoes and peas.
The harvest is in.
The hay is in the barn.
Zzzz.
The sun has set and
now it is time for bed.
The farmer goes to sleep.
What a busy year
on the farm!

Farms Around the World

Corn is used in cooking oil and cornmeal.

Bananas grow on trees in plantations.

Sunflower seeds make cooking oil.

Oranges grow on trees in groves.

Cocoa beans are made into chocolate.

Rice grows in flooded fields.

Let's Grow Potatoes

You will need:

- seed potatoes, sprouting
- very large pot with holes and small stones in the bottom
- soil
- water and plant food

1 Half-fill the pot with soil. Place five potatoes just below the soil with shoots upward.

2 Each time the shoots appear, cover with more soil until the pot is full.

3 Keep the soil well watered, remove weeds, and add plant food every few weeks.

4 Either pull up the potatoes when the plant flowers, or let the leaves die back to have bigger potatoes.

41

Farm Tractors

Each type of tractor is useful for doing a different job.

Plow

Tractors with plows churn up the soil.

Sprayer

Tractors with sprayers water the plants.

Baler

Tractors with balers press crops into bales.

Farm Quiz

1. Where on the farm do the pigs live?

2. What did the farmer collect from the hens?

3. Which baby's dad is a bull?

4. What happens to sheep's woolly coats in the summer?

5. Name two things milk can be made into.

Answers on page 45.

43

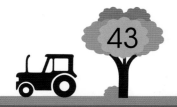

Glossary

churn turn and mix

dairy foods made from milk

hay dried grass

hopper this holds the seeds of wheat (grain)

orchard place where fruit trees grow

plantation large group of the same kind of plant

stalk tall part of a plant

straw dried stalks of grain

Index

Answers to the Farm Quiz:
1. Pigsty; **2.** Eggs; **3.** Calf;
4. They get sheared;
5. Check answer on page 30.

Guide for Parents

DK Readers is a four-level interactive reading adventure series for children, developing the habit of reading widely for both pleasure and information. These books have an exciting main narrative interspersed with a range of reading genres to suit your child's reading ability, as required by the Common Core State Standards. Each book is designed to develop your child's reading skills, fluency, grammar awareness, and comprehension in order to build confidence and engagement when reading.

Ready for a *Beginning to Read* book

YOUR CHILD SHOULD

- be familiar with using beginning letter sounds and context clues to figure out unfamiliar words.
- be aware of the need for a slight pause at commas and a longer one at periods.
- alter his/her expression for questions and exclamations.

A VALUABLE AND SHARED READING EXPERIENCE

For many children, reading requires much effort, but adult participation can make this both fun and easier. So here are a few tips on how to use this book with your child.

TIP 1 Check out the contents together before your child begins:

- read the text about the book on the back cover.
- flip through the book and stop to chat about the contents page together to heighten your child's interest and expectation.
- make use of unfamiliar or difficult words on the page in a brief discussion.
- chat about the nonfiction reading features used in the book, such as headings, captions, recipes, lists, or charts.

46

TIP 2 Support your child as he/she reads the story pages:

• give the book to your child to read and turn the pages.

• where necessary, encourage your child to break a word into syllables, sound out each one, and then flow the syllables together. Ask him/her to reread the sentence to check the meaning.

• when there's a question mark or an exclamation mark, encourage your child to vary his/her voice as he/she reads the sentence. Demonstrate how to do this if it is helpful.

TIP 3 Chat at the end of each page:

• the factual pages tend to be more difficult than the story pages, and are designed to be shared with your child.

• ask questions about the text and the meaning of the words used. These help to develop comprehension skills and awareness of the language used.

A FEW ADDITIONAL TIPS

• Always encourage your child to try reading difficult words by themselves. Praise any self-corrections, for example, "I like the way you sounded out that word and then changed the way you said it to make sense."

• Try to read together every day. Reading little and often is best. These books are divided into manageable chapters for one reading session. However, after 10 minutes, only keep going if your child wants to read on.

• Read other books of different types to your child just for enjoyment and information.

Series consultant, **Dr. Linda Gambrell**, Distinguished Professor of Education at Clemson University, has served as President of the National Reading Conference, the College Reading Association, and the International Reading Association. She is also reading consultant for the **DK Adventures**.

Have you read these other great books from DK?

BEGINNING TO READ ①

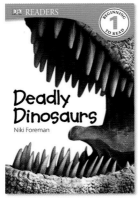

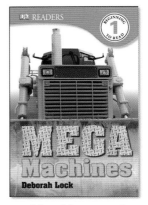

Roar! Thud! Meet the dinosaurs. Who do you think is the deadliest?

Holly's dream has come true— she gets her very own puppy.

Hard hats on! Watch the busy machines build a new school.

BEGINNING TO READ ALONE ②

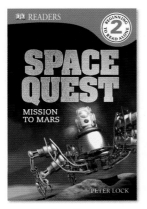

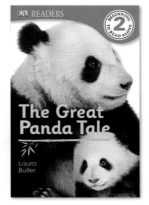

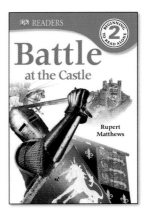

Embark on a mission to explore the solar system. First stop—Mars.

Join Louise at the zoo, preparing to welcome a new panda baby.

Discover life in a medieval castle during peacetime and war.